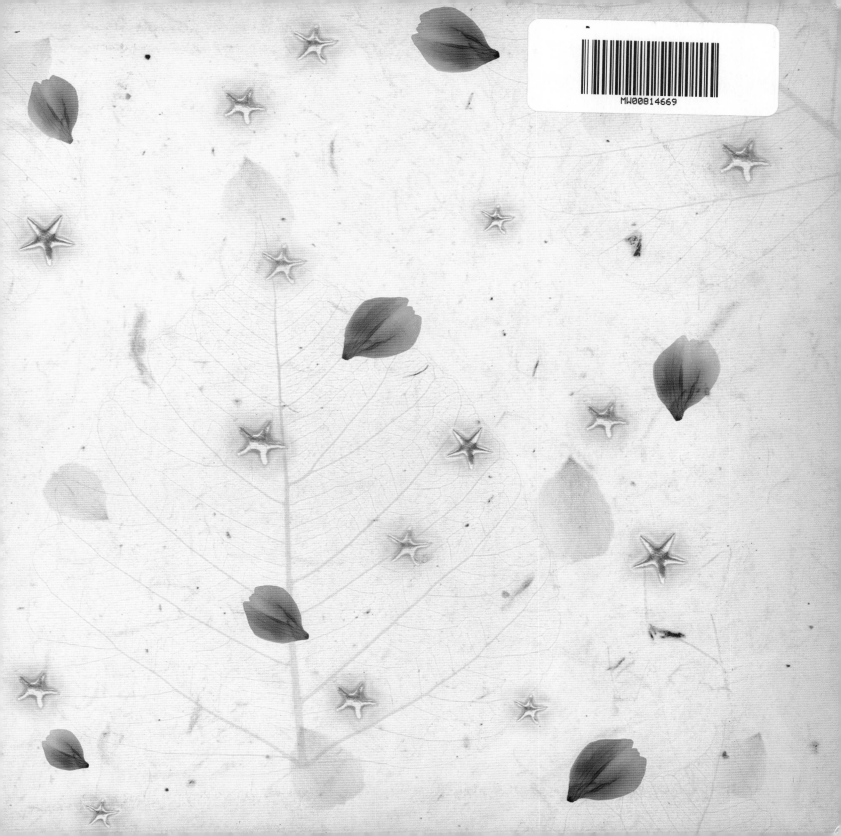

FREDERICK WARNE
Published by the Penguin Group
Penguin Books Ltd, 80 Strand, London WC2R 0RL, England
Penguin Young Readers Group, 345 Hudson Street,
New York, New York 10014, USA
Australia, Canada, India, New Zealand, South Africa

This edition first published by Frederick Warne 2007

Printed in China

Flower Fairies™

Stories from the Garden

Contents

A Flower Fairy Valentine's Day

Today is a special day. The Crocus Fairies
are up first. "It's Valentine's Day!" they
shout as they wake the other fairies up.

Red Clover sees her friend the bee. "Happy Valentine's Day," she whispers.

Michaelmas sees his friend the butterfly. "Happy Valentine's Day!" he says.

"I wonder whether
I will get a card,"
thinks Forget-me-not.

"I have one
for you,"
says Privet.

Beech Tree
has made a card
for his best fairy
friend, Elder.

To my dear friend Elder
I'd just like to say
Happy Valentine's Day!
Love, Beech

x x x

Celandine is clutching a Valentine card for Jack-go-to-bed-at-noon. "I have a Valentine's card for you," she calls.

Jack-go-to-bed-at-noon
blows her a petal kiss
to say thank you.

Periwinkle makes a card for Tulip.

Dear Tulip,
So happy you're my friend
And so to you I send
A Valentine that's blue
With pretty blue flowers, too.

Love, Periwinkle

x x x

At the end of the day,
everyone in Flower Fairyland
has a Valentine Card,
but there is one left,
who can it be for?

It's one for you!

A Flower Fairy Springtime Dance

Deep in the garden,
a fairy is being chosen
to perform the opening
song and dance at the
Springtime Festival.

Beautiful voices and tapping
toes can be heard all around.
Eventually, it's little Narcissus
Fairy's turn.

Shy Narcissus takes her place
in the clearing, as the light
from a hundred stars shines
down upon her.

Her twinkling toes skip delicately across the glade. It is soon decided that she will have the starring role at the festival.

The fairies disappear into the dusk, leaving the Narcissus Fairy alone. "Am I really going to perform in front of all the fairies in the garden?" she asks a surprised grasshopper.

She suddenly feels frightened, so she picks
up her velvety skirt and runs to the
darkest part of the flowerbed.

The day of the festival dawns
and the fairies are so excited.
"Where is Narcissus?" asks the Celandine
Fairy. "She's the most important fairy
of the day!" adds Daisy.

The Rose-Bay Willow-Herb
Fairy flys off to search for
her, but Narcissus is
nowhere to be seen.

The Crocus Fairies skip down to the pond.
"Have you seen Narcissus?" they ask
a fairy who lives nearby, but there
had been no sign of her.

At last, a passing butterfly spies Narcissus. "You must fly to the festival or you'll be late!" says the butterfly. "But I'm scared of singing and dancing on my own," whispers Narcissus.

"You'll be fine. I'll be there to watch over you," the butterfly cries. Narcissus feels much braver and soon agrees to perform.

Just as the festival begins, the smiling Narcissus Fairy confidently skips into the clearing and begins to sing and dance beautifully.

The pretty butterfly is by her side. She isn't alone after all!

At the end of the song, the fairies clap and cheer and Narcissus doesn't feel afraid anymore. She is the proudest and happiest fairy at the festival.

Her fairy friends join in the singing and dancing, and the Springtime Festival is enjoyed by all in Flower Fairyland!

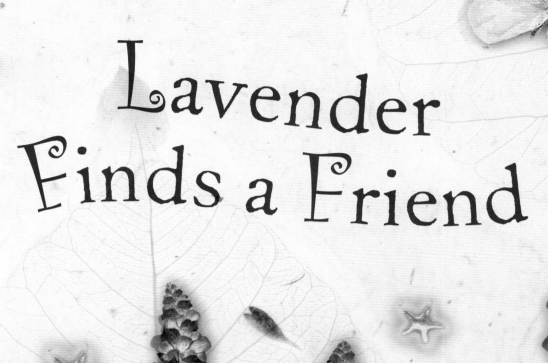

Lavender
Finds a Friend

Hidden amongst the leaves
and blossoms in the garden,
the flower fairies live quietly.
At night, they come out to play!

In the morning, a sleepy Lavender is the first to wake up. She has lots to do! She sings to the other garden fairies, to wake them up, too!

Lavender's blue diddle, diddle—
Lavender's green;
I'll scent the clothes diddle diddle
Put away clean—
Clean from the wash, diddle diddle,
Hanky and sheet;
Lavender's spikes, diddle diddle,
Make them all sweet.

When Lavender
has a minute to spare,
she writes in
her diary:

Dear Diary,

Today I have been busy
washing the fairies' clothes.
I have made some soft
Lavender soap

and I scrub away at the stains. I wonder what some of the fairies get up to – their clothes are so dirty!

Once Lavender finishes washing
the fairies' clothes, she hangs them
up on the line to dry.
"Your bonnet is beautifully scented!"
says Sweet Pea Fairy to her sister.

One day, in the garden,
Lavender hears two fairy
friends laughing together.

"I wish I had a best friend of my own," Lavender thinks.

That evening
Lavender writes
in her diary:

Dear Diary,

I'm sad tonight.
Every day I wash and
scent the fairies' clothes,
but I never

have time to make
any friends. My only
friends are the white
butterflies who visit each day
to drink Lavender nectar.

Whatever shall I do?

"I know what I'll do,
I'll make a friendly fairy spell,"
says Lavender.
This is what
she puts in it:

a dash of
fairy dust

a drop
of dew

a whisper
of moon sparkle

a tiny fairy
giggle

a sprinkle of
Lavender petals

Lavender casts the spell and
waits to see who will come…

Out steps Cornflower from the flowerbed. "I'll be your friend!" he says.

"Me too!" calls Foxglove from behind her.

"And me," says Snapdragon.

Lavender laughs.

"What a wonderful spell!" she says.

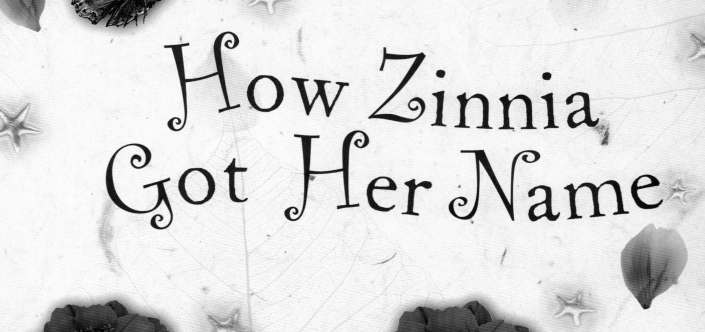

How Zinnia Got Her Name

In Flower Fairyland, every fairy has a flower and every flower has a fairy.

All the fairies except one. And because she doesn't have a flower, she doesn't have a name. "If I don't find a flower soon," the little fairy says sadly, "I will have to leave Flower Fairyland."

Sweet Chestnut, a kind-hearted Flower Fairy, overhears the little fairy crying and takes pity on her. He throws her a chestnut with a note inside. "Catch this, little fairy," he shouts.

To be a Flower Fairy you must:
1. Learn to dance
2. Learn to sew fairy costumes out of petals
3. Learn to look after plants and flowers

"When you have learnt these lessons, Wild Rose – the oldest and wisest of the Flower Fairies – will present you with a flower," Sweet Chestnut adds.

The little fairy whizzes over to where Columbine lives. Columbine is teaching a friend to dance.

The little fairy doesn't want to disturb them, so she hides in the tall grass, learning all the steps by heart.

Next stop is Tansy. She is the best seamstress in all of Flower Fairyland. Tansy is sewing a yellow dress made out of petals.

The little fairy watches her intently, and she soon knows all the little stitches Tansy uses.

Next the little fairy learns
the most important lesson
of all – how to look
after her plant!

Shirley Poppy is expert at
sowing her seeds far and wide.

Sister Pink is in charge of
trimming her flower's petals
and brother Pink is in
charge of the leaves
and stalks.

That night the little fairy
writes in her diary:

Dear Diary,
Today I learnt how
to dance by watching
dainty Columbine practising.
I learnt how to sew
Flower Fairy costumes
from Tansy.

And Poppy, along
with brother and sister Pink,
taught me how to care for
a plant. I have learnt all of the
Flower Fairy lessons and tomorrow
I will ask Wild Rose if I can
have a flower of my own…

The next day, Wild Rose decides the little fairy is ready. "Your magical flower name is... Zinnia!" she announces.

Zinnia is thrilled to have
a flower of her own.
"At last!" she says. "Now
I have a home in Flower
Fairyland!"

Wild Cherry's Secret

High up above us, the
Flower Fairies of the trees
leap and swing.

These fairies dangle
daringly from their
branches, singing and
calling to one another.

All except one. Beautiful Wild Cherry
Blossom sits quietly, watching the others.

"Come and play
with us!" calls
cousin Cherry.
But Wild Cherry
shakes her head,
and clutches
her branch.

Beech Tree notices that
she looks a little scared.
"What's wrong?"
he calls out to her.
But Wild Cherry
doesn't answer.

That evening Wild Cherry
writes in her diary:

Dear Diary,

All the other tree fairies

are such good climbers,

but I don't think

I'll ever be a real fairy acrobat.

The others are beginning to notice that I never join in. What should I do?

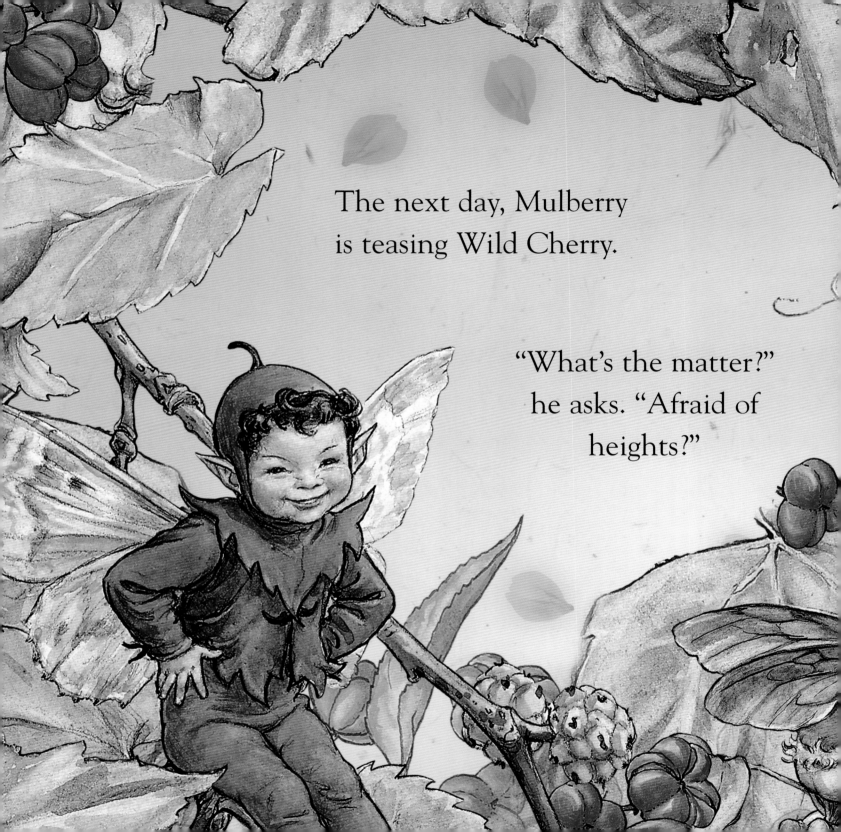

The next day, Mulberry
is teasing Wild Cherry.

"What's the matter?"
he asks. "Afraid of
heights?"

"Don't worry,"
says Sweet Pea.
"I love you! And so do
the other babies. You
always watch over us."

Just as daylight begins to fade, there is a cry from somewhere above the fairies' heads. Without anybody noticing, Baby Apple Blossom has climbed far too high...

...She's stuck!

Everyone rushes to help. "Just take my hand," says Lime Tree.

Crab-apple holds out her skirts and calls up from below. "Jump!"

But the little baby cries
for the one she really
wants – her aunt,
Wild Cherry.

Quick as a flash, Wild
Cherry climbs to the rescue.
She scoops up the tearful
baby, and sets her safely
on a lower branch.

All the Flower Fairies are cheering, as Wild Cherry suddenly realizes what she has done. She beams proudly.

That night,
Wild Cherry writes
in her diary:

Dear Diary,

I am proud that I

rescued baby Apple Blossom.

But that's all the leaping

about I want to do.

I think I am the kind of fairy who likes to keep to the low branches and that's ok with me!

Rose Plays Hide and Seek

One beautiful summer's day, Rose calls to all her fairy friends. "Come and play hide-and-seek with me!"

"What a lovely idea!" says Strawberry. "I've got a special prize for the winner. It's red and sweet and delicious! Can you guess what it is?"

Fairy friends soon flutter around to play the game.

"Buzzzz!" says Bumble Bee from a nearby flower.
"Can I join in? I'm very good at hiding."

"Of course," laughs Rose.
"We'll all try to find you,
then it'll be someone else's
turn to hide!"

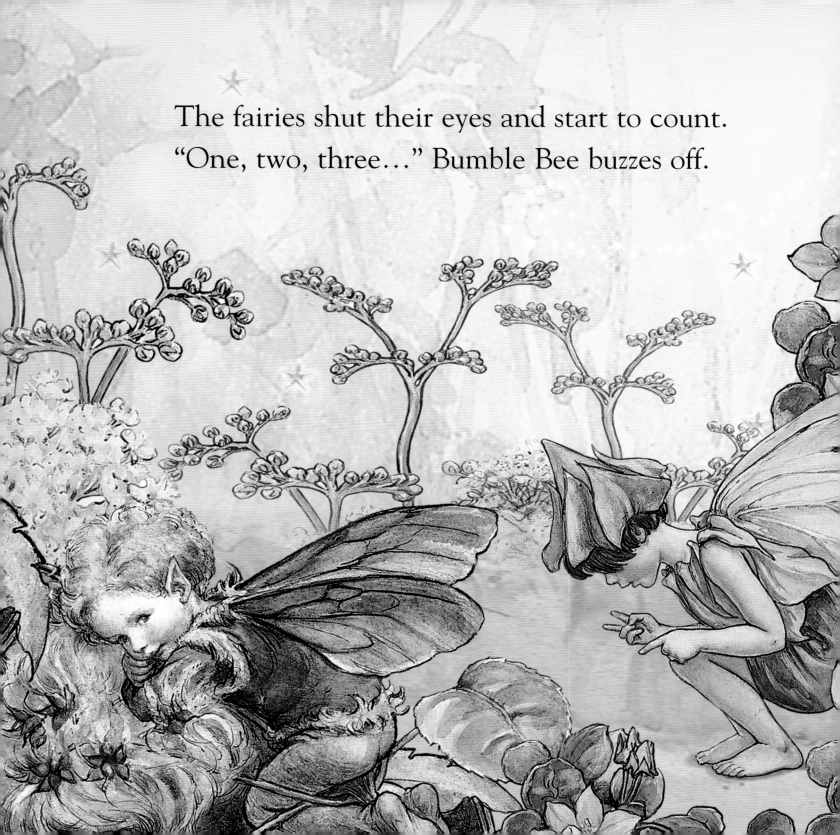

The fairies shut their eyes and start to count.
"One, two, three…" Bumble Bee buzzes off.

"No peeping!" he reminds the fairies.

"…forty-five,
forty-six, forty-seven…"

Nightshade feels something soft brush past his cheek, but he remembers to keep his eyes shut.

He counts out loud to help the little fairies who can't count such big numbers yet.

"...ninety-nine, one hundred! Ready or not! Here we come!"

The fairies fly off to find their friend Bumble Bee. They look everywhere! But Bumble Bee just can't be found.

"Have you seen our friend?" Michaelmas Daisy asks a passing butterfly.

"Here he is! I've won, I've won!" calls an excited fairy, pointing to a pretty plant.

But Beech Tree
smiles and shakes his
head. "That's not
a bee. It's a
flower that
looks like a bee!
Keep looking, everyone!"

The fairies look everywhere, but no one can find Bumble Bee.

Then Scilla has a clever idea. "If we can't find him with our eyes, we'll use our ears!" he says. "Let's just be quiet and listen. Bumble Bee always buzzes when he's happy!"

Sure enough, there's a buzzing sound coming from a nearby flower.

"Found you!" laughs Snapdragon, spotting the busy bee.

"Snapdragon is the winner," cries Strawberry, "but I think everyone deserves a prize. Come and help yourselves!"

The fairies and Bumble Bee enjoy a delicious picnic of strawberries and honey in acorn cups.

"Mmmm! Hiding is fun, but finding is even better!" laughs little Rose.

Pansy
Makes New Friends

There is a family of Flower Fairies hiding in every garden. These graceful little creatures are careful to stay out of sight, but if you are lucky you might just spot one tiptoeing amongst the flower beds.

As soon as they feel the first light of
the morning, the Garden Fairies come
out to play. They can't wait to dance
and spin amongst the bright sunbeams.

Pansy leads the way, unfurling her
brilliant petals to soak
up the warm sunshine.

One evening Pansy writes
in her diary:

Dear Diary,
I had such fun today
with Poppy and Cornflower.
We twirled and skipped
until we couldn't take
another step. I so
adore playing in the
summer sunshine!

But where does the
sun go at night?
Tomorrow I'll follow its
golden rays out of the garden
until I discover where it lives.
What a magical place
that must be!

Pansy sets off at dawn, waving goodbye to her
fairy friends. The sun is already twinkling
through the morning dew in the meadow.
The wild flowers are turning their
tiny heads up to greet the day.
"I'm Buttercup," says a pretty
yellow fairy with a bright smile.

"And I'm Sow Thistle!" laughs another.
"Would you like to play with us?"
Pansy would love to, but she
can't stop. "Sorry not today,"
she smiles. "The sun is climbing
up into the sky and I really must
try to follow!"

Soon it's midday and the
sun is shining high in the sky. Pansy flies
into a nearby wood. She flits up to the top
branches, where some Tree Fairies are chattering.
"I'm off to visit the sun, is it far from here?"
she asks. Mulberry bursts into ripples of fairy
giggles. "Your little wings won't reach the sun!"

"You can sit next to me!"
says Poplar, pointing to his
white fluffy branch. "My seeds
make the fluffiest fairy cushions."
"No thank you," replies Pansy. "I can't
see the sunlight through all these leaves!"

By sunset, Pansy arrives at a peaceful
stream. "You must be tired," says Willow.
"Come and dip your feet
in the cool water with me."

To her amazement,
Pansy spots the sun
glittering on the
pool's surface.
Iris smiles as
Pansy leaps in
with a huge splash!

Later on, Pansy dries off her wings in the fading rays of sunlight, and writes her friends a postcard.

Dear Garden Fairies,

I finally thought I had found the sun, but it just turned out to be a reflection! Where will it lead me next? I've already visited beautiful meadows, enchanted treetops and mysterious waters. The sun still keeps moving in the sky – hope I find my answer before nightfall!

See you very soon, love

Pansy xx

The Garden Fairies

Third Flower Bed

Through the Green Grass

Inside the Secret Garden

When the sun finally tucks
itself away behind the
horizon, Pansy skips back
to her own magical garden!

"Pansy's home!"
cries Honeysuckle.

"Welcome back, Pansy," the fairies cry.
"Did you find what you were
searching for?"
"Oh yes!" Pansy beams.
"I followed the sun and it led
me to a magical place – back
here to my fairy friends!"

Blackthorn's Changing Seasons

Every fairy in Flower
Fairyland loves one season
more than any other.

Some love spring or
summer, when pretty
petals open in the sun.

Others enjoy the
ripe fruits and golden
leaves of autumn.

Winter is magical
too, with sparkling
frosts and beautiful,
bare branches.

Blackthorn thinks she likes
early spring best of all.

"I love to feel the gentle sun on my
face," she smiles. "Spring makes
everyone happy!"

"It makes us want to dance!" her friends
the Crocus Fairies agree.

Day after day, more flowers open their petals
and show their pretty faces to the sun. Soon
Flower Fairyland is full of beautiful blossoms.

Gradually, spring is turning into summer.

"Perhaps summer is the best season after all," says Blackthorn.

Blackthorn loves to watch
the little fairies having fun
in the warm breeze.

Suddenly, she notices
something. Pretty white
petals are fluttering all
around her.

"Oh no!" she cries.
"Some of my flowers
are blowing away!
Come back!"

"Don't worry, Blackthorn!"
says kind Forget-me-not.
"Each season brings
new surprises. You'll see."

Blackthorn is not so
sure. She looks at her
branches and sighs. It is
a long time before spring
will come again!

The weeks go by.
One warm summer's
evening, Blackthorn
watches sadly as
Willow dips her toes
in the stream.

"How lovely your
long, green leaves are,
Willow," she says.

"You have lovely
leaves, too, Blackthorn!"
laughs Willow.

Blackthorn is surprised, but it is true! Forget-me-not was right. Everything changes – even pretty little fairies.

Autumn comes. Who is
this little fairy smiling
shyly amongst the leaves?
How pretty she looks!
It's Blackthorn!

She has a lovely new dress,
and her branches are full
of wild plums, called sloes.

"I am so happy that
autumn is here!" she cries.
"And I can't wait for
winter, too. Then my fruits
will be sweeter and ready
to eat."

Blackthorn's fairy friends are so happy for her. Lots of them have tasty nuts and berries, too.

"Which is your favourite season now?" asks Rose Hip.

"All of them!" laughs Blackthorn. "It's lovely all year round in Flower Fairyland!"

Buttercup
Goes to the Ball

In amongst the waving grasses
at the edges of the meadows
the Flower Fairies make their
homes, under the tall stems
of their plants.

One of the pretty meadow fairies
is Buttercup. On the first day
of summer, she wakes up early
and shakes out her lovely wings.
She greets the day with a song.

'Tis I whom children love the best;
My wealth is all for them;
For them is set each glossy cup
Upon each sturdy stem.

O little playmates whom I love!
The sky is summer-blue,
And meadows full of buttercups
Are spread abroad for you.

Buttercup's friend, Poppy,
has a brilliant idea.
"Let's have a Summer Ball!"
she says.

The little grass fairies decide
to announce the Ball.
"It will be a night to remember!"
says Cotton-Grass grandly.
(Just to make sure, every
fairy's invitation is sealed
with a Forget-me-not flower.)

Buttercup keeps a diary.
Her pen is made from
a dried grass stalk.

Dear Diary,

Today I polished my

golden buttercups

until they shone,

and trimmed
and t*i*d*i*ed my leaves.
I want to look my best
for the Summer Ball!

All the Flower Fairies try
on their best party clothes.
But one sad little fairy has
nothing to wear. "I'll lend
you something," says Vetch
kindly...

The night before the
Ball, Buttercup writes
in her diary:

Dear Diary,

Everyone is talking

about the Ball and

practising their dance steps.

The Summer Ball is a
great success. All the
younger fairies stay
up late!

After dancing all night,
Buttercup is one of the
last fairies to leave.
"I can't wait for the
next Ball!" she says.

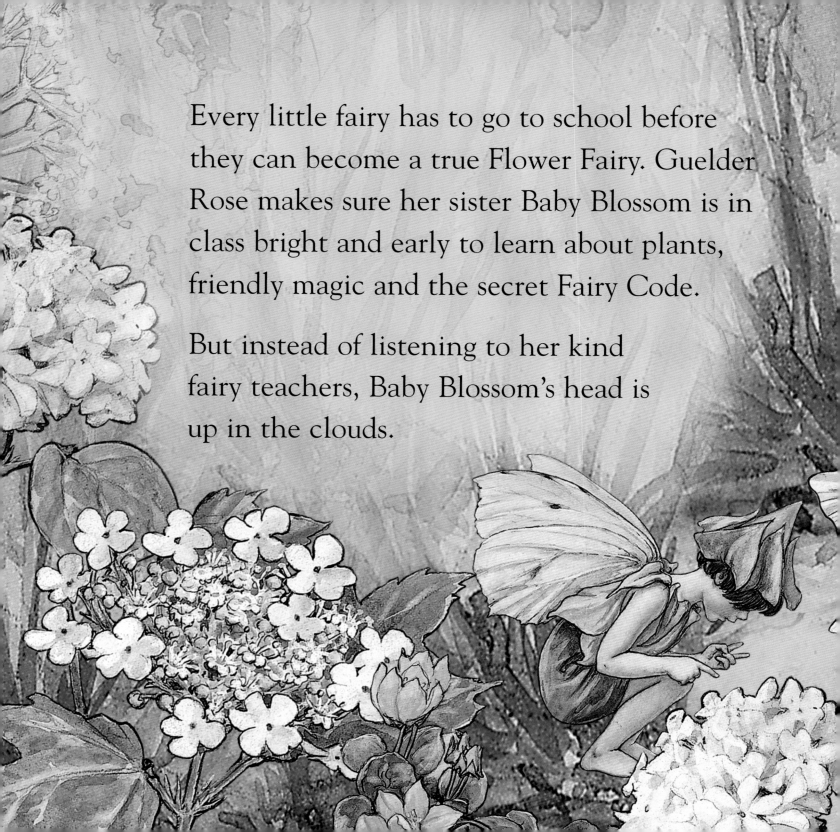

Every little fairy has to go to school before they can become a true Flower Fairy. Guelder Rose makes sure her sister Baby Blossom is in class bright and early to learn about plants, friendly magic and the secret Fairy Code.

But instead of listening to her kind fairy teachers, Baby Blossom's head is up in the clouds.

That evening she writes in her diary:

Dear Diary,
My sister says I must try harder with my lessons, but I long to be up in the trees with the older fairies. All day I dream of playing in the branches and chasing the butterflies!

Tomorrow I must learn how to make fairy wishes. I so want to wish, but how will I ever manage it if I can't sit still? I must try my very best and make my sister proud!

Jack-go-to-bed-at-noon arrives at daybreak to teach the young fairies how to wish. Baby Blossom and her friends watch carefully.

"I catch the first
breeze of the morning,"
he tells them, puffing up
his cheeks and blowing
hard. "The wind carries
the wishes far and
wide, spreading
my magic
like fairy dust."

Then Christmas Tree fairy shows
them how she weaves her wonderful
spells. "I close my eyes, let my
wings sparkle and tap my wand
twice," she says. "You each have
to discover your own special
way of wishing."

But while the other little fairies listen
closely, Baby Blossom has fluttered away.

By the time she has finished daydreaming, the class is busy practising wishes down in the meadow. She hurries to catch them up, and then she gets started. She has lots of things to wish for.

Baby Blossom closes her eyes and taps
the twig twice, but nothing happens!

The poor fairy can't
understand what
has gone wrong.

Later Guelder Rose and the older fairies stay up whispering in the starlight. "Maybe your little sister needs some friendly fairy help," suggests Nightshade. "I heard Baby Blossom crying because she's bottom of the wishing class."

"Let me sprinkle a special dream spell onto her pillow," says Poppy.

Here is Poppy's spell:

Before you can make fairy magic, you must discover your own way of wishing. Ask the Wishing Flower to help you. Sweet dreams, Baby Blossom!

Baby Blossom seeks out the beautiful white Wishing Flower as soon as she wakes up.

"You're an enchanting little Tree Fairy who loves to skip and float from leaf to leaf," sings the Flower. "Remember this and all your wishes will come true."

In class, the fairies are learning to fly.
Baby Blossom looks up at the treetops
and wishes as hard as she can.
Suddenly she floats up in the air,
using her white blossom branch
as a delicate parachute.

"I'm a true fairy at last!"
she gasps. "Guelder Rose
will be so proud."

A Flower Fairy Christmas

The Flower Fairies
love Christmas.
For some of them it is the
busiest time of the year!

Holly seems to be
everywhere at once!
He wants everyone
to join in the fun.

"I've got a great idea!" he says.
"Let's have a surprise party for
the Christmas Tree Fairy!
She has so much to do
at this time of the year."

The young fairies are
very excited and start
thinking about the
party right away!

Holly sends beautiful invitations to everyone.

Dear Fairy,

Merry Christmas!

Come to our party on Christmas Eve by the Christmas Tree. Please bring something for everyone to enjoy.

Love from Holly xx

P.S. Don't tell the Christmas Tree Fairy. It's a special surprise for her!

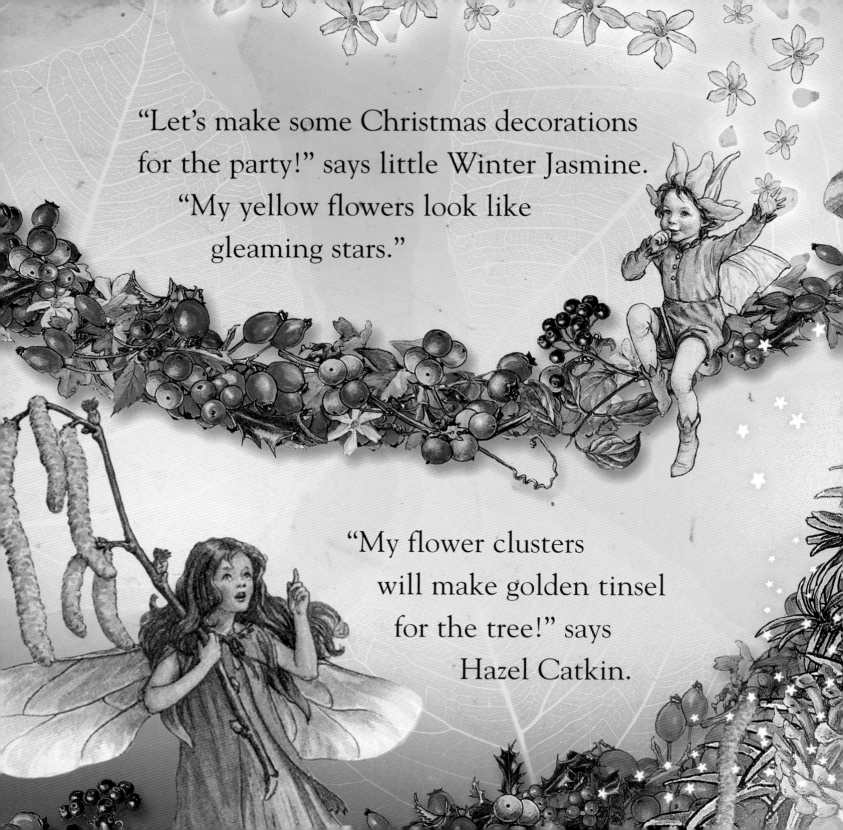

"Let's make some Christmas decorations for the party!" says little Winter Jasmine. "My yellow flowers look like gleaming stars."

"My flower clusters will make golden tinsel for the tree!" says Hazel Catkin.

Pine Tree brings cones to
paint and sprinkle with
sparkling fairy dust.

Heather brings streamers
of bright winter berries
strung together.

Some of the fairies decide to make delicious food and drink for the party.

"I'll make some yummy berry juice!" says Blackberry.

"I'll bring my special seed pies," says Mallow.

"Baked apples will be a tasty treat!" calls Crab-apple.

"And I'll bring acorn cups for the blackberry juice!" says Acorn.

"Let's practise some Christmas music!" suggests little Winter Aconite. "I'll be the conductor!"

Listen to those seeds, "Rattle! Rattle!"

The poppy seeds go "Shhh! Shhh!"

The bugle makes a very
loud noise, "Toot! Toot!"

Hear those Christmas
bells, "Ding-a-ling!"

The fairies play Christmas
carols. The sound is so jolly
that everyone starts to dance!

It's Christmas Eve and
nearly time for the party.
The fairy friends catch
moonbeams and starshine
to light their lanterns.

"We're nearly there!" cries Burdock.
"I'm so excited!"

"Sssshhhh!"
says Cotton-Grass.
"Let's all flutter up together to
surprise the Christmas Tree Fairy!"

"Merry Christmas!" call the fairies as they greet their friend on the Christmas tree.

"Look what we've brought!"

With happy faces, the fairies bring their decorations and tasty treats to the Christmas Tree Fairy.

"Thank you! Thank you!" she cries.

When the tree was
decorated it looked
beautiful. All the fairies
danced around,
and began to sing:

"We wish you a Merry Christmas!
We wish you a Merry Christmas!
We wish you a Merry Christmas!
And a Happy New Year!"

A Merry Christmas to
you too, from all your
Flower Fairy friends.